RICH LEGEND

RICH LEGEND

The Secrets of the Five Golden Coins of Ancient Egypt Revealed

DAMRONG PINKOON

JAICO PUBLISHING HOUSE

Ahmedabad Bangalore Bhopal Bhubaneswar Chennai
Delhi Hyderabad Kolkata Lucknow Mumbai

Published by Jaico Publishing House
A-2 Jash Chambers, 7-A Sir Phirozshah Mehta Road
Fort, Mumbai - 400 001
jaicopub@jaicobooks.com
www.jaicobooks.com

Published in arrangement with
Damrong Pinkoon Company Limited
999 Gaysorn Plaza 5th Floor, Lumpini
Pathumwan, Bangkok 10330, Thailand

RICH LEGEND
ISBN 978-81-8495-671-9

First Jaico Impression: 2015

Printed by
Rashmi Graphics
#3, Amrutwel CHS Ltd., C.S. #50/74
Ganesh Galli, Lalbaug, Mumbai - 400 012
E-mail: rashmigraphics84@gmail.com

RICH LEGEND

The Top Secrets of Billionaires
Who Possessed
The Most Gold in Ancient Egypt

Author's Preface

Rich Legend
is a guide to running a successful business.

A story arose in ***ancient Egypt***
that used the metaphor of a young man
who looked for efficient ways
to run a successful business.

At first, he only wished to survive.

However, he eventually became a secure
and wealthy businessman.

Only a few principles to get rich
exist. According to the Egyptian tales
in this book, the reader who perceives
the essence of these tales
and is able to put them into practice
can make a lot of money.

The author fully hopes that every reader
will find at least a few helpful and attention
worthy ideas in this book.

RICH LEGEND

Publisher's Preface

Many people who started
from scratch become rich.

These people have successfully
turned their small businesses
into successful and lucrative companies.

Even someone with little education
and scarce funds can succeed in business.

On the flip side, people with a higher education,
sufficient funds and parental support,
can still fail.

So, what really determines
their success or failure?

The simple principles of doing business
and pragmatic ways of amassing gold
from the times of ancient Egypt can lead
us to wealth without too many difficulties.

Contents

		Page
Chapter 1	Millionaire, ka-lae, the owner of five secret golden coins	8
Chapter 2	The right answer is waiting for a good question	18
Chapter 3	The three magicians	48
Chapter 4	The first lesson of a businessman	58
Chapter 5	The second business lesson is expense	92
Chapter 6	The third lesson is profit	142
Chapter 7	The last lesson from the three old men	178
Chapter 8	Five coins	188

RICH LEGEND

Millionaire, Ka-Lae,

The Owner of

Five Secret Golden Coins.

The glory of ancient Egypt brought about much trade.

However, both among the poor and rich, only a few people were aware of the real secrets of wealth.

When ancient Egypt was ruled by the King Pharaoh, trade flourished tremendously. Various kinds of commodities were available such as herbs, precious items and clothes that were imported from different Egyptian towns.

Livestock was common and people freely consumed goat milk and mutton. They raised cows, ducks and geese. Their livelihood improved and trading looked promising. Merchants thrived and rapidly became rich.

The kingdom's social hierarchy was divided into three categories and included the upper, middle and working classes.

Among the three classes, the upper class earned the superior social status. It consisted of royal families, civil servants, senior priests, physicians and other aristocrats. Merchants and artisans belonged to the middle class.

The biggest group included unskilled laborers, servants and slaves, who were considered the lowest in the population.

Most able-bodied men preferred to serve the Pharaoh by becoming his military assistants. Those who were not the sons of aristocrats worked in food shops. While those who were robust opened weapon-making businesses, which required a lot of strength and skill in order make swords or fabricate armor.

Meanwhile, women sold various merchandise that came from Nubia, a town in southern Egypt. Besides this, they also sold flowers plucked from many miles away. Children started working at the age of seven or eight. Their work was varied and included grooming camels, taking care of babies, milking goats, scaring off birds for farmers and looking after shops.

Furthermore, locals processed Egyptian papyrus into various kinds of materials such as utensils fuel, houses and baskets. More importantly, paper was produced from papyrus and used to record information and special events. Hence, the widely known papyrus paper was born.

Business was brisk. Merchants moved freely to exchange exotic goods at the central marketplace and hardly took a day off.

What they wanted were gold coins. Every trader wanted more of them including Magga, a young man who was loved by all villagers.

Magga was a really good boy of the village. He worked like the others. He noticed that when the other boys got paid, they went to Aunty Filly's to drink fermented fruit juice. At the end of the night, the boys would only have a few golden coins left.

Magga decided to earn more money by selling fermented fruit juice. His business began to thrive and he decorated his shop with fresh fruits.

While the business flourished, Magga wondered why the gold coins that he procured gradually dwindled in volume.

Thus, he decided to go and see the millionaire, Ka-Lae, who was also his loyal customer, to understand his lack of gold coins.

Magga entered Ka-Lae's towering castle and went to the drawing room where he looked around in admiration. It was the first time he had seen so many glittering golden ornaments; he felt like he was in a palace.

Woven curtains painted with golden gilds, golden spirit jugs and golden cups were on display everywhere. Even Ka-Lae's maids covered their faces with radiant golden veils.

The millionaire sat in his favorite chair, which was decorated with fancy golden arm supports.

"Your Excellency, my business has encountered a little problem. I request you to purchase some fruit from me with gold coins. If I don't get the gold coins from you, then nobody will supply fruit to me. The most important raw material," Magga pleaded.

"Should I help you or not?" Ka-Lae responded.

"I came here to ask a favor of you. I would really appreciate your kindness if you help me," Magga humbly implored the millionaire.

"Sorry, I don't find the need to give you what you ask. Moreover, I don't need to receive gratitude from anyone," the millionaire replied haughtily.

"Please, what can I do so that so that you will help me?" Magga asked.

The millionaire chuckled and said, "I will give you one chance. I will answer a question. If you give me the correct question to my answer, you will soon have countless gold coins. But remember, I will do that only when you ask me the right question that corresponds to my answer."

"And what if I ask you a wrong question?" Magga enquired.

"Tomorrow, before the sun sets, you must come here and ask me your question. It is your only chance," the millionaire concluded before turning away and going back to his chamber.

Magga, a shrewd young man suddenly felt confounded because he had no idea how to ask a question that could satisfy the millionaire. As he walked home, he considered his options thoughtfully. He recalled a story about how Ka-Lae became a millionaire.

It was said that when Ka-Lae was very young, he earned his living by milking goats, fixing camel shoes and selling water bags made from leather to tourists and the many merchants that passed through his town.

Later that evening, Magga approached the kind and friendly, Aunty Ronnie, who owned a camel farm. He decided to ask her about the millionaire's true history.

He listened intently and learned the same story all over again.

"A long time ago, when Ka-Lae was just a little boy, he worked as the other boys worked. He hammered shoes into camel hoofs, cleaned and washed the animals and their stables. He made a lot of money because there were numerous merchants that passed through his town.

Then, Ka-Lae suddenly disappeared from the village. Before he left, he paid me a visit. He asked me how he could earn gold coins all the time," recalled Aunty Ronnie.

"And what did you say to him?" Magga asked.

"I told him I had no idea. I only spend what I have," Aunty Ronnie replied.

"After that, Ka-Lae left the village and stayed away for many years. When he returned home, he started his business again. His business gradually flourished and he became rich. He got richer by the day until he became the richest man in our town, a millionaire," Aunty Ronnie added.

"Thank you very much, Aunty. I will make sure I come back and see you again," Magga said and went back home.

The next day, he spent all his time mulling over what he had learned from Aunty Ronnie. He kept thinking of the question that would make the millionaire Ka-Lae give him gold. He yearned for the correct question and the consequent answer he was looking for.

RICH LEGEND

2

The Right Answer is Waiting For a Good Question.

If you want to know
the secrets of wealth,
you need to have
strong determination and patience.

The next morning the young man, armed with shoes for camels, bags made from leather and all the gold coins he had, came back to see Ka-Lae.

"You've come back earlier than I anticipated," Ka-Lae greeted Magga.

He began, "I once obtained gold coins by changing the shoes for the merchants' camels and selling water bags to tourists. After that, I did many jobs until I settled down to run a fermented fruit juice shop. I've been working since I was a boy. All my gold coins are in this bag," he said with a steely determination. Then, he posed his good question.

"Could you please tell me how I earn gold coins like you once did?"

"Hah! You really got it," the kind millionaire happily laughed out loud.

"I've already prepared something for you," the millionaire said, picking up a perforated wooden box beside him.

"Inside this box, there is an invaluable item that I've kept since I was young. I've made many journeys in the quest of an answer. What I discovered, on my journeys I have kept in this wooden box. In all my travels, there was only one thing I searched for and that was how I could earn gold coins all the time. Then I got this thing," the millionaire passed the box to Magga.

The young man felt excited as it was the first time he was receiving something from the hand of a millionaire. He thought to himself, "Is this what turned Ka-Lae into the wealthiest person in town?"

The young man gently unlocked the box and opened it. He found a map inside with five gold coins drawn on it with different obverses.

The obverse of each coin featured a symbol while the reverses depicted a symbol resembling a letter. But he could not figure the meaning of each different symbol.

"This is a map I prepared in order to give someone who needs to see the three magicians who were once my masters. They played a vital role in changing my life. They can give you the answer to the meaning of these five coins they gave me a long time ago."

"They told me to give these coins to the right person. You have to bring these five coins to the Pund region, where the three magicians will have you take many tests."

"If you pass their tests, the three magicians will teach you how to run a profitable business. After that, you can find the answer to your question with your own abilities," the millionaire said.

"What do they look like?" Magga asked excitedly.

"What tests do I have to go through?"

"You ought to know only what you should do. That is enough," the millionaire said.

"If you want to know more, you better set out as quickly as possible," Ka-Lae suggested.

"Yes, sir. I feel grateful to you. I will begin my trip at dawn tomorrow," the young man truly appreciated the millionaire's special gift.

"I want to ask you one last thing. Am I the first person to receive this special gift from you?" He asked curiously.

"You are absolutely right to ask me this. Many people have come only to ask for gold coins but no one wanted to know how I managed to earn so many of them. I gave them the same choice as I gave you. But nobody wanted to learn; they never asked me what you did. They simply wanted to loan some gold coins," the millionaire explained before saying farewell to the determined young man.

"I hope you find what you are looking for," Ka-Lae finally said.

"I'd like to express my heartfelt thanks to you. I will try my best to find the truth and return home as soon as possible." The young man said goodbye to the millionaire with much gratitude in his heart.

How can I earn gold coins frequently like you once did?
Hah! You really got it.

The wooden box with a map to the Pund region and five gold coins.

That night, Magga closely observed and attentively scrutinized the coins. He wondered whether these coins were responsible to have made Ka-Lae a millionaire. He believed there was something hidden behind these mysterious coins, and was eager to learn the meaning of the symbols on the coins.

He knew that he had to find the secret to knowledge and the secrets of success as quickly as possible.

Though he was well aware that it would not be easy to acquire the knowledge required, he did not fear any difficulty or any possible encumbrance.

He then began to write his thoughts on the papyrus paper:

Business requires knowledge,
which has to be pursued.

It takes more than a day to enrich your mind.

It is not that easy to gain knowledge.

Knowledge can be accumulated
on a daily basis.

It can be somewhat hard to pursue it.

To pursue knowledge requires patience.

If we give up half way, we will gain nothing.

If we lose patience, we will earn nothing.

Determination is required to
achieve a goal.

And achieving that goal means success.

The Secrets of the Five Golden Coins

The next morning, as the first light of the day shone through Magga's window, it revealed his luggage and other traveling gadgets in the corner of the room. Magga left the fermented fruit shop to his older sister, Moomild, so that she could supervise it. He then bid farewell to his younger sister, Minna.

"I hope to soon find what I am looking for and come back before you grow up to be an adult," Magga said to Minna, his pretty younger sister.

"I will return as soon as possible to give you a hand. Please take care of Minna," the young man said, as he bid farewell to Moomild.

Heading to the Mysterious Pund Region

This was the first time Magga had traveled out of his village. He did so with firm resolution to discover the secrets of the five gold coins. He was determined that he would not return home to his family until he was successful in his mission.

Before mounting his camel, he wrote something on a papyrus paper to help his conscience mind before commencing his trip. He wrote:

Business is a journey.

The weather is scorching some days,
while storms are seen on others.

It may rain on some days,
while on other days we may
need more water.

We may also need more food on some days.

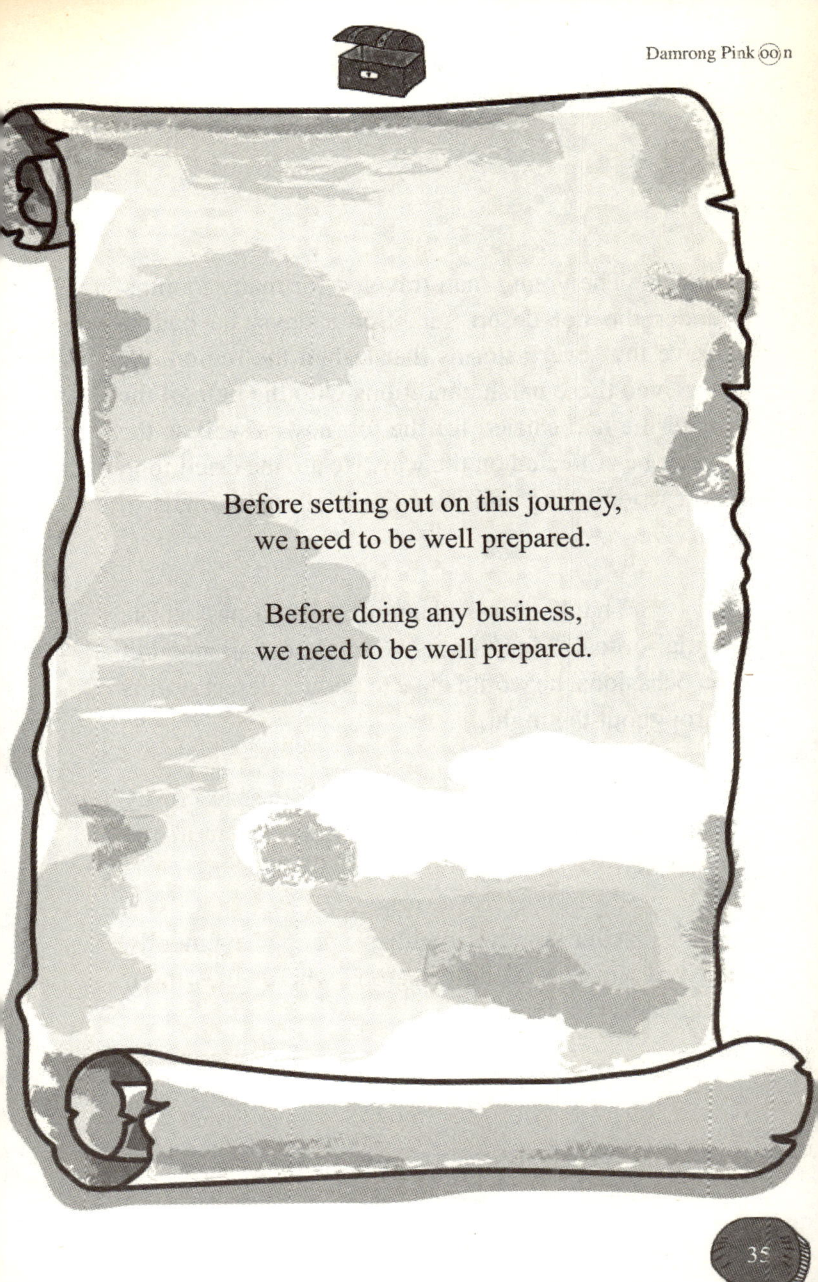

Before setting out on this journey,
we need to be well prepared.

Before doing any business,
we need to be well prepared.

The young man traveled for many months, under the hot desert sun. Some days, he had to brave the severe storms that lashed the region. He survived these harsh conditions with the help of the water he had carried for the journey as well as the water he collected on the way. He ate the dried food he carried along and later even hunted animals to survive.

Thanks to his planning, Magga passed the initial ordeal. Most nights were almost silence but on occasions, he would have to endure desert storms throughout the night.

He made his way out of the desert by following the Sirius star, the brightest star in the night sky.

After many months, Magga eventually arrived in the Pund Region where the three magicians resided.

Magga looked back at his journey so far, and wrote on a piece of papyrus paper the following.

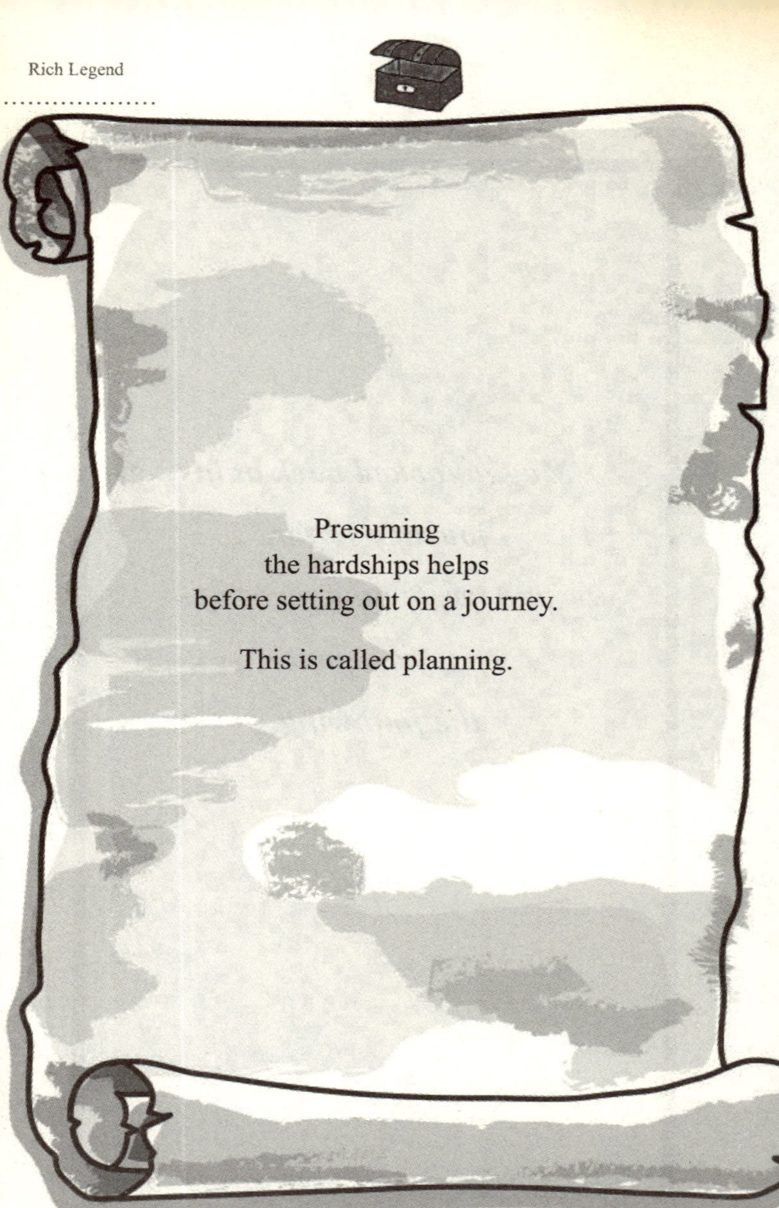

Presuming
the hardships helps
before setting out on a journey.

This is called planning.

Presuming
the possible hurdles that will be
encountered before doing business
is called planning.

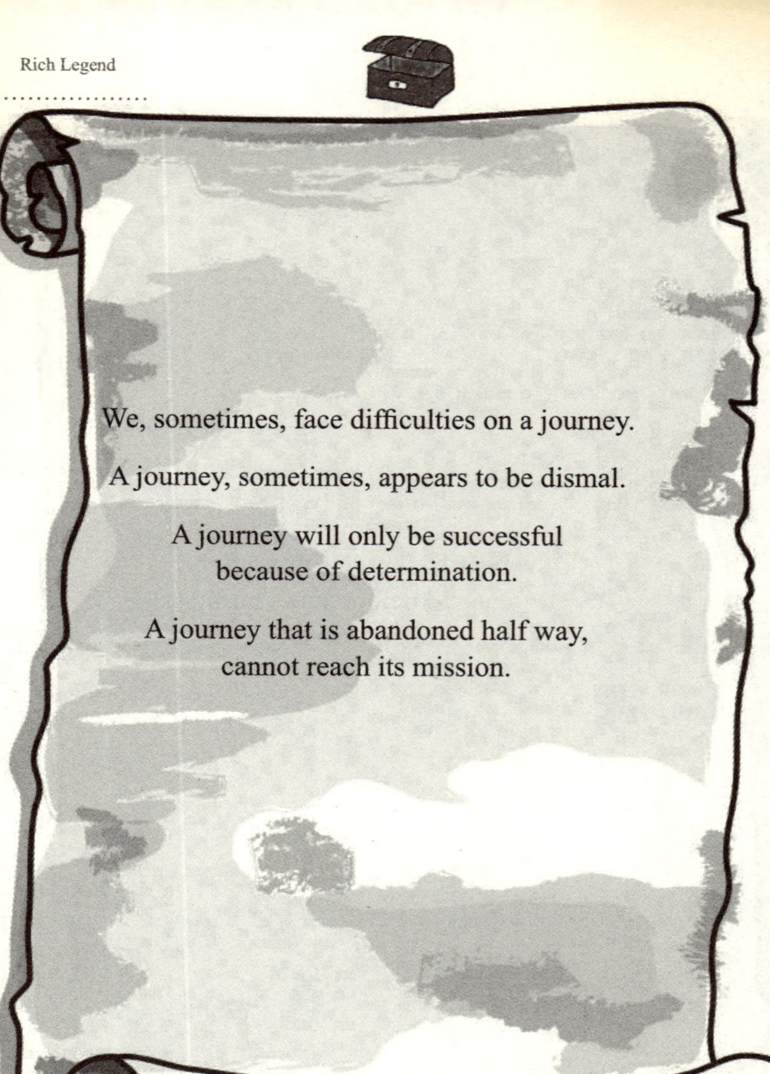

We, sometimes, face difficulties on a journey.

A journey, sometimes, appears to be dismal.

A journey will only be successful
because of determination.

A journey that is abandoned half way,
cannot reach its mission.

Doing business will cause a lot of difficulties.

Business can, sometimes, look dismal.

A business will only succeed
because of determination.

Business that is given up half way,
will not succeed.

Magga had traveled many months to pursue the knowledge required by him to run a successful business. He wandered while trying to evade the ever-present desert storms. He trudged through the scorching desert with great difficulty.

When he arrived at the border of the Pund Region, he was immensely delighted. He expressed his inner feelings by writing on the papyrus paper the following:

The more we overcome obstacles,
the more we are proud of ourselves.

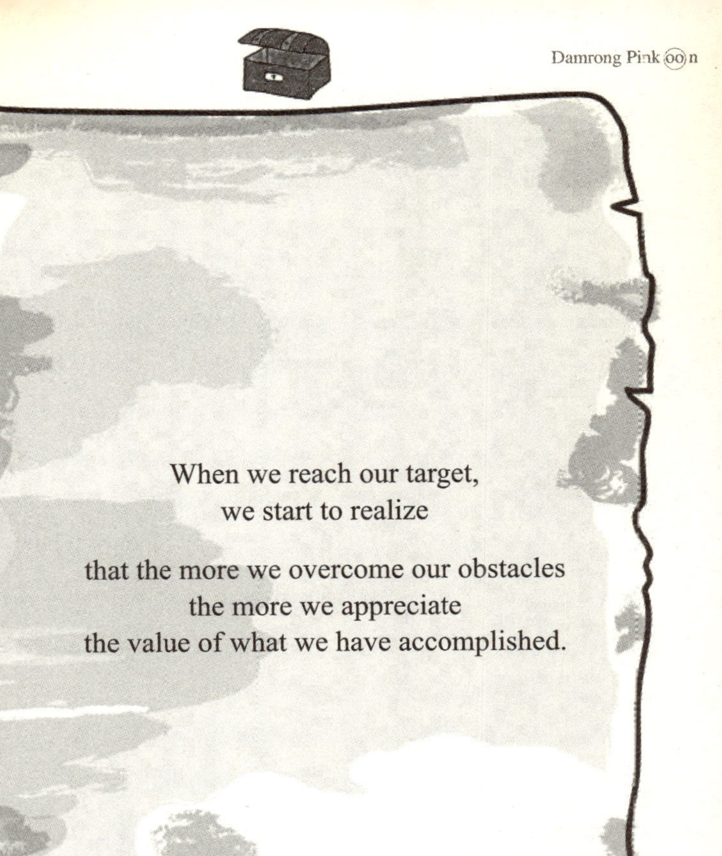

When we reach our target,
we start to realize

that the more we overcome our obstacles
the more we appreciate
the value of what we have accomplished.

A winner
never gives up.

The one

who gives up

never wins.

RICH LEGEND

3

The Three Magicians.

Magga went through a large door and halted under a large tree, where he saw the three elderly magicians in conversation. They were joyfully speaking to one another.

The young man moved closer to the group. He glanced at one of them and saw a coin with the symbol **S** hanging around his neck. The coin resembled the same coin he had with him.

He didn't dare to interrupt their conversation, so he turned around and saw a **huge stone** on which was written:

Pund Region

Business is like riding a tiger.

It is easy to start but difficult to quit.

If you fall from the tiger, you will be injured.

The ones who fall are badly hurt or even die.

There are many different ways in life.

Let destiny lead us:

Second, we select our own life and path.

At crossroads, we can select left or right,

the decision lies in the way you think.

One path is full of roses.

Another is scattered with thorns

and moving vines.

It is dirty and dangerous.

Go along the road you like,

it is your choice.

In the beginning, business might be difficult.
But later, it will start to become
easier right to the end.
If you set your heart on it earnestly,
even thorns may become flowers.

Lazy people should not choose the business road.
Whingers should not use the road of merchants.
Negative thinkers should not
walk along the business street.
It's hard for them to succeed in life.

Diligent and determined people can go anywhere.
Positive thinkers and creative thinkers
work well in their jobs and link.

If you select this path,
you should stay true to it.
You must love your own way
and love yourself.

Shortly, the three old men stopped talking and turned their attention to the young man.

"What have you come here for, young boy?" one of the old men asked.

"My name is Magga. I received five golden coins from a millionaire called Ka-Lae. He asked me to come to the Pund Region to meet the three magicians who were his masters. Here are the five gold coins," the young man said and opened his hand to show them the five coins.

"I should think you are quite exhausted after your long journey," another old man said.

"Yes, I have been away from my home for over six months," said Magga.

"This is the Pund Region but there are no magicians here. There are only the three of us who come here frequently; we are simply ordinary people. We did meet Ka-Lae many years ago. We had a conversation together. Yet, we are not his masters."

"I saw a coin with the S symbol hanging around your neck; just like the one I have," Magga explained.

"Is the coin with the letter S on it a symbol?" He then asked.

"It is mine. It represents the initial letter of my name, which is Sa-Les."

One of the men replied, "The man called Otutu possesses the coins C, E and M."

Otutu was bald and perhaps the most conspicuous of the group. The third one was the youngest. He was plump and smiled to laugh a lot. He seemed to be all the time happy.

"His name is Profito." Sa-Les said.

Then, he asked Magga,

"Why do you want to know the secrets of five gold coins?"

"I have been a businessman since I was young. I have experienced many trials and tribulations. My business was risky on some days but stagnant on others. And so, I became more and more impoverished. As days passed, I decided to go and see the millionaire Ka-Lae. He told me to keep these coins with me and to go and see the three magicians at the Molin School, where I could learn the secrets of wealth like he had. That is why I came here to meet the three of you," explained Magga.

"Before doing business, you need to learn a lot of things. If you feel tired, would you still choose to continue?" One of them asked.

"I have already chosen this path, so I will keep fighting till the end. I do not want to quit." Magga said confidently.

"Good. Rest tonight, tomorrow morning come see us here and we will teach you how to do business based on our own experiences. After all, you deserve this after your long journey."

"Thank you very much, sir," Magga said greatefully.

He made his way to the hotel where he would stay the night. He was extremely worn out, and so he went to bed early, and slept peacefully.

RICH LEGEND

4

The First Lesson of a Businessman.

The following morning, the Magga returned to see the three old men at the same location as the previous night.

"Good morning, masters," said Magga.

"Good morning. Did you well sleep last night?" the old men inquired.

"Yes, very well, sirs," replied Magga.

"Let's begin," one of them said.

"I will start with a tale. A long time ago, there were two Nubian merchants who came to our village. The first merchant brought cotton fabric and linen with golden embroidery, along with food for sale."

"This food was a round and flat-shaped dough that could be fried on a hot pan. When the dough was well cooked, it would be coated with goat milk and then with honey. It was called Bayu."

"The first merchant noticed that the villagers dressed only in completely white outfits without any golden embroidery. Moreover, they did not eat 'Bayu'. After thinking about this situation, he decided to leave our town for another place where people needed his goods."

"Meanwhile, a second merchant brought the same commodities to be sold in the village. They were cotton and various colored linens with golden embroidery and 'Bayu'".

"He noticed that the villagers did not have these kind of things. He was filled with extreme delight. Thus, he decided to settle down in the village. Gradually, his business began to flourish."

"Whenever the villagers wanted to use cotton fabric and linens with golden embroidery, they would think of this Nubian merchant. And if anyone wanted to eat some exotic food, they would come to him. This generated wealth for the Nubian merchant who later became a millionaire."

"What did you learn from this tale?" the old man finally asked.

"I think these two merchants have totally different points of view in terms of opportunities and obstacles," Magga replied.

"The first one saw that this town did not use the goods he was selling. So, he thought that was an obstacle to his trade. It was better for him to go to other villages where they used these kinds of things so he that could easily sell them."

The dough Bayu with Honey.

Customer groups are people in general.

Ah. It's like this.

It focuses on the demonstration of all manufacturing procedures and reasonable prices.

Profito

"But the second merchant saw that this town did not use the goods he was selling. He saw this as a good opportunity to be successful."

"Congratulations, you're right," the man explained.

"The second merchant had a sense of real merchandising. He viewed an obstacle as an opportunity in stark contrast to the first merchant, who viewed the opportunity as an obstacle."

Magga had listened attentively before he took out a piece of papyrus paper to record what he just learned from the first of the three old men; he wrote:

A winner
always sees a situation as an opportunity,
even if he faces an obstacle.

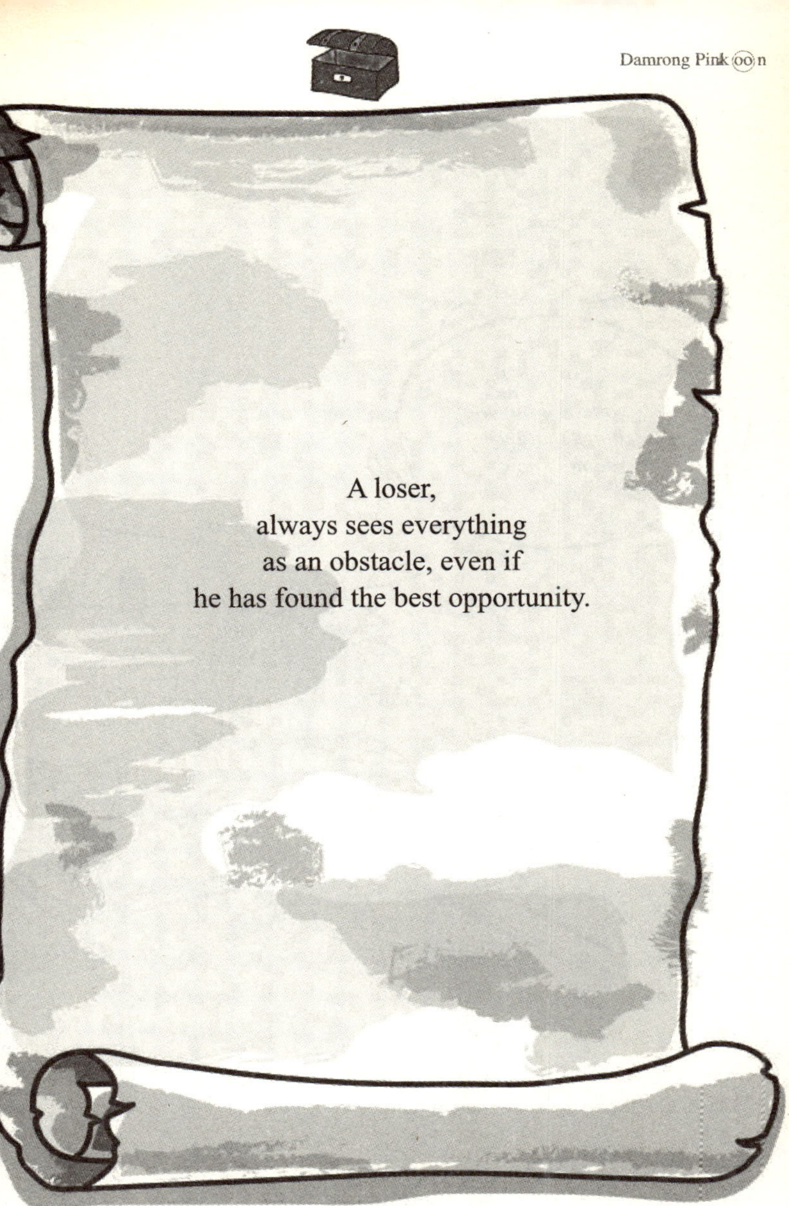

A loser,
always sees everything
as an obstacle, even if
he has found the best opportunity.

The first merchant

The second merchant

"There is something more. The second merchant seemed to sell different things in the village. But in reality, he always sold the same items that turned out to be exotic and unique in the market. Many customers suddenly showed interest in linens with colored embroidery and started to eat 'Bayu' which became a new and popular taste in town."

"However, the most important aspect was that he had no rivals. At the heart of all of these business moves was the symbol, S, abbreviated from my name SA-LES."

The most important aspect
for a business
is
SALES.

SALES

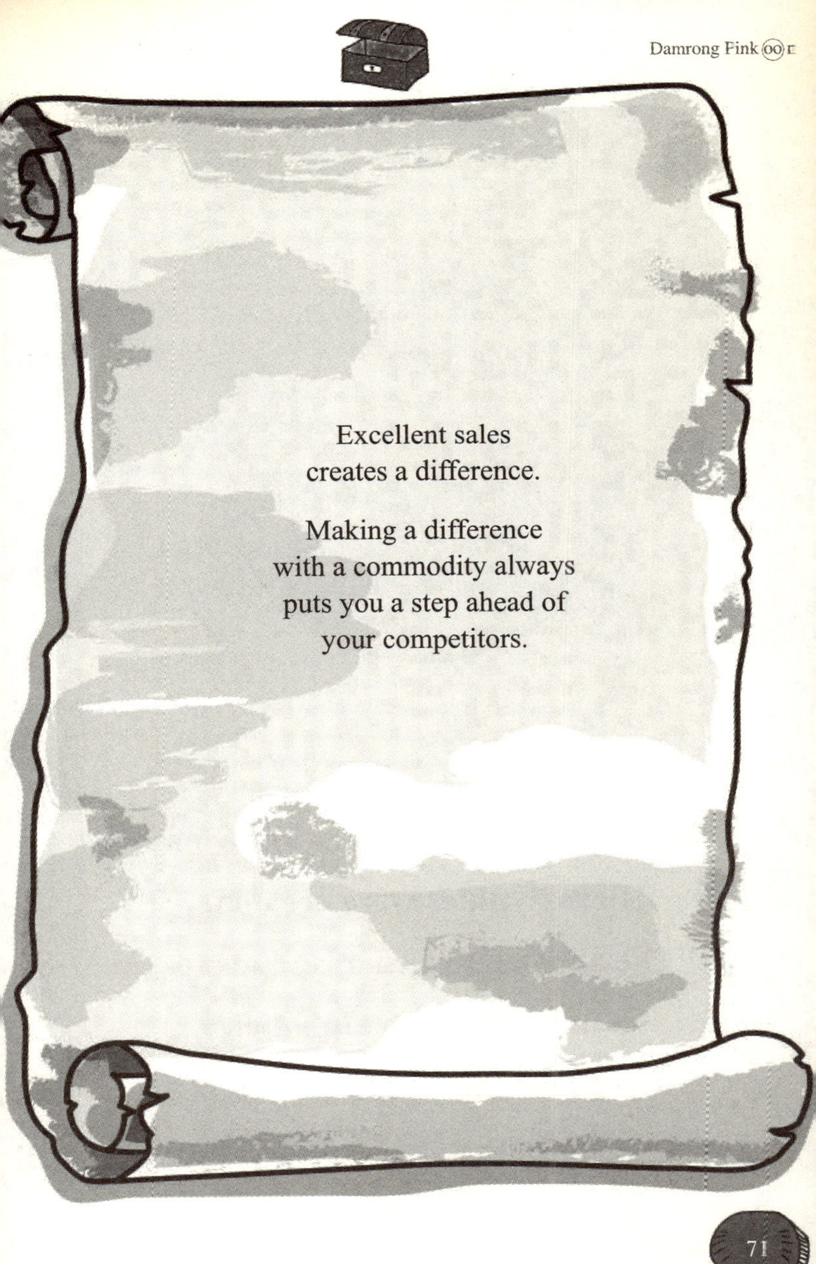

Excellent sales
creates a difference.

Making a difference
with a commodity always
puts you a step ahead of
your competitors.

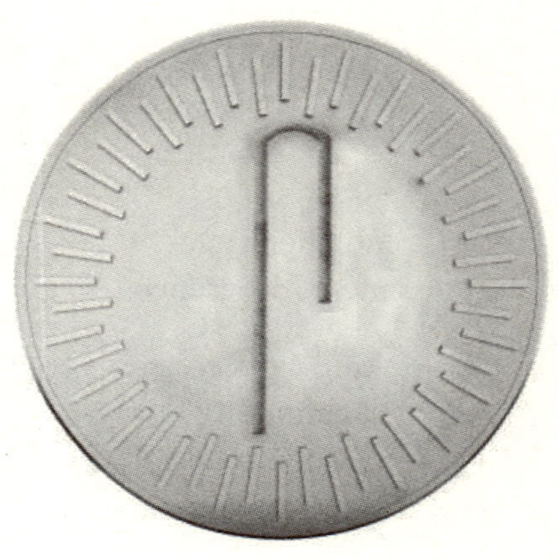

In Ancient Egypt, letters known as Hieroglyphics were created. The above letter corresponds to S in the English alphabet.

In the English alphabet, the letter S on a coin means SALES.

Sa-Les said, "The second Nubian merchant in this tale was me. Initially, when I started my business, I faced a lot of problems. And then, after I met my two dear friends, Otutu and Profito, we discussed and exchanged our business ideas. They helped me unravel the puzzles about how to run a successful business. Later on, what we had talked about created riches and wealth for all of us."

"What were the difficult tasks or problems in your story?" Magga asked.

"When I started my business, I had several problems just like other merchants did. I could not distinguish my customers and what I had to do. It was not until my two dear friends gave me some precious advice that I was able to win a big deal of selling a huge quantity of merchandise in a short period of time."

"Could you explain this to me?" Magga asked.

"Sure. You will soon know everything necessary to run a successful business. You have traveled a long way to be here, so you certainly deserve to know all there is to it." Sa-Les said.

"When I started to sell my two main products, I wanted to sell as much cotton fabric and linens with golden embroidery as I could." Sa-Les explained.

"I set a low price and put my goods down on the pavement at the marketplace. I hoped that people would be interested in my goods right from the beginning. But not a single piece could be sold."

"Besides I thought I could sell more Bayu if I redecorated my shop and set a high price. I hired many children to help serve my customers. But unfortunately, no one dared try to a new and exotic food. Eventually, my hopes of becoming a millionaire began to fade." Sa-Les explained his situations.

"But when I met my two dear friends, they gave me some advice, which tremendously helped to improve my business."

Even though I sell my goods at low prices. Why does nobody want to buy them?

"The advice they gave me was about customers. They told me that my embroidered linens could be sold to only some people, not everyone. Some women might have been interested in trying it, but not every woman."

"According to their cultural practice, all women were dressed only in white. And it was hard for them to change their well-established culture and dress in embroidered and colored linen." Sa-Les explained.

"My friends also said that if I sold a small volume of merchandise and sold it only to a particular group of customers, I needed to embellish my shop to make it more beautiful so that it would be in accordance with the beautiful merchandise on display."

"It was inappropriate to display my commodities on the ground. Besides, any commodity that could be sold only to a specific group of customers could be sold at a higher price. This would attract people's attention more."

Sa-les continued, “If I wanted people to feel good about my products, I had to approach a few pretty women in the village and give them embroidered linens for free. Then, I would ask them to wear this fabric and walk around the town to show off my products at least once a week.”

“I tried to follow all the advice my friends had given me. That created a tremendously positive change in my business; quite a reversal of fortune.”

“The two or three pretty women, whom I gave the embroidered linen to, walked in the marketplace and suddenly aroused attention of passers-by because they were dressed differently from the others who were clad only in white clothes.” Sa-Les explained.

“People approached them to ask where they purchased this graceful silk. They replied that it came from my shop. After that many young girls rushed to my shop to buy my goods and I quickly ran out of stock.”

"Furthermore, some men came to buy my products and gave it to their wives or beloved ones as a present."

"As for my Bayu business, my friends advised me that my dough could be sold to people of all ages. Therefore, there was no need to elegantly adorn my shop. The way in which we produced and cooked Bayu was quite interesting."

"When people saw how it was made, they wanted to try it. The important thing was that I had to sell it to many people in large volumes. I could not set a high price, just an appropriate or reasonable one, so that many people would be interested and make a quick decision in buying it," Sa-Les elaborated.

"So, I changed where I sold my products. I put the cotton and embroidered linens on display inside the shop and sold the Bayu dough in front of the shop. This displayed the manufacturing process, from kneading and shaping the flour to coating it with goat milk and honey very well."

"Due to its fragrance and cheap price, people who passed by stopped and wanted to try the Bayu. Moreover, they also told others to taste it. Soon, all the villagers came to buy it."

"We can compare trade to a good start. A business depends on the starting point. A good start is always an advantage."

"There are many people who start a business they like and eventually succeed and are happy with it. That is surely double luck. But it is not always true that everyone can be successful in the business they love."

Ladies are a target group.

Beautiful products.

Beautify the front of your shop and sell your products at a higher price.

It's just that!

Otutu

The Bayu dough is really delicious.
Please try it!
Why do people walk away even though they can try it for free?

Sa-Les continued talking,

"There is no fixed formula for success in every business.

Even though you remember whatever you have done successfully in the past won't mean that you will succeed in the future by following the same strategy."

*"To do business, you must be first armed with principles and the right guidelines.
Then you can apply them.
Each business has its own style,
its own model."*

*"Sometimes, the same type of business can start and run in different areas.
It still needs different strategies that must be used at the right time and place."*

"In conclusion, success consists of many different factors depending on what your products are, who uses them, who to use it with, where it is used, when it is useful, how it can be purchased and why people need to buy it."

*"Being successful in a city with a certain method does not mean that you can be successful in another city.
Your strategy might fail if you do not study all the details."*

"The first factor of a successful business is basically sales. Sales is the first step of a good start in competition. If sales fare well, we can look at other such factors important cost and expenses. At the end of the day, everyone who does business always hopes to earn profit."

"Well, that's it for today, we are now finished. We will continue tomorrow with Otutu and Profito, will talk to you the day after tomorrow," Sa-Les concluded his important lesson.

Before bidding farewell to the three old men, Magga wrote what he learned on a piece of papyrus paper:

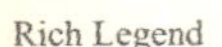

Before doing business
we need to know who our customers
are and how to make them
interested in our products.

We need to set a suitable price
for each particular target group.

If the goods are well allocated,
we can sell them at a higher price.

To do what we like does not
always guarantee success.

Before doing business,
we need to have principles,
knowledge and the right guidelines.

The same business conducted
in a different place
or at a different time might require a
different strategy to achieve its goals.

A Loser's Life

....

Many people like to do business.

Some people start as employees.

The loser starts work and because he earns only a little money, gets bored.

He then starts to look for a new job.

The loser starts to work without planning.

He gets discouraged easily.

Some losers adjust themselves by begging the sky and earth for help.

Some losers who fail get discouraged again and again.

A Winner's Life

Many people like to do business.

Some people start as employees.

The winner starts from a job he loves.

The winner does better at work,
has a good plan, and
enjoys working.

The winner enjoys life.

The winner adjusts
by pursuing knowledge.

The winner succeeds,
has a stable career
and expands his enterprise
with more power.

The young man left the three old men and headed towards the town. The market of the town was bustling as usual. There were many sellers, including merchants from other towns.

Magga noticed an exotic fruit that could not be found in his town. Big boys came here to help the adults search for gold. On his way, he glanced at a big workshop where many blacksmiths were busy working. This place was widely known as Otutu Sword Smiths.

The young man wondered whether this enterprise belonged to Otutu, who he had just met. So he approached the head of the blacksmiths and asked him.

He was right to assume. The old man Otutu received orders from King Pharaoh to make swords, shields and armor plates for the royal guards so they could use them during war.

After Magga had gathered the information, he went back to his lodge. He laid in bed thinking about what the old man would teach him tomorrow.

The most important thing in trading is sales.

RICH LEGEND

5

The Second Business Lesson is Expense.

Knowledge can be acquired every day.

The next day, Magga came to see the three old men again.

The young man told them about his visit to Otutu's shop.

"Yes, that's my enterprise. I will take it as an example to teach and explain to you the significance of the other three coins; C, E and M." Otutu said.

"Yesterday, you learned about sales. That is not enough to make you rich. The other issues that are equally important are cost and expense."

"Most people know about cost, but few very understand it. To do business, one needs to know more about cost. Otherwise, the chance of your business surviving is slim or zero."

In Ancient Egypt, letters known as

Hieroglyphics were created.

The above letter corresponds to

C in the English alphabet.

In the English alphabet,

the letter C,

as on this coin, means

COST.

"All right, let's get started. When you have to produce something, you need raw materials. At my store, I also have to buy steel, charcoal and wood for fuel, hammers and other equipment so that my workers can make swords.

Do you think there are any other raw materials than these other ones I've mentioned?"

"I don't think there are any more," Otutu asked.

"There is still another, it is called manpower cost," Magga replied.

Otutu smiled and said, "Manpower cost, what does it mean?" Magga seemed confused.

"Everyone who comes to work will receive a wage for their daily expenses, including myself because I have to eat and spend like others."

"But you do not work there," the young fellow asked.

"No. Even though I am the owner of the sword smith, I have my own burdens, and personal expenses, so I have to use the money from my business."

Magga began to understand, he said that means everyone who is involved in the enterprise is entitled to a wage payment. That's what you called manpower cost, right?"

"That's right. Most people think that it's enough to sell products with a slightly higher price than the purchase price. But those people forget that they also put their personal wage in the enterprise."

"Moreover, some family members take assets from the enterprise for their own use, which is unwittingly excluded from the human cost. If they continue like this for a long time their business will surely start to go down. And if no one can pinpoint the cause, then the enterprise can end up shutting down."

"If we take all these factors into account, the product cost will be higher accordingly, won't it?" Magga asked.

"Yes, it's true. You need to be aware of the real data about your enterprise to be successful. If you have wrong knowledge, your actions will be erroneous. So, you will not succeed in the future." Otutu replied.

"I didn't know this, not until I received an order from King Pharaoh's commander-in-chief to make swords for the palace," confessed Otutu.

"Before selling the swords to the palace, I started a small blacksmiths shop in the town. In the market, there were three blacksmith, shops one belonged to me and the two other shops were bigger competitors."

"The three shops always received my orders from the palace to make good quality swords for the soldiers. Initially, the soldiers of King Pharaoh used the weapons manufactured in a weapon-making department in the palace."

"But they could not produce enough weapons on time, because many new soldiers were being recruited. Finally, orders began to come to our three shops," the old man took out a sword and looked at it.

The more income
you receive,
the more expenses
you will have.

He then said, "Due to the large volumes of orders, we expanded our enterprise until each shop had 30 to 40 blacksmiths. A few years passed, we became wealthy but we still worked very hard.

Another ten years passed and only my enterprise remained," said Otutu.

"Why? The three shops regularly received orders from the palace. Why did the other shops stop business?" asked Magga.

Bills!

"They did not want to close their enterprises but there was a turning point over the cost and expenses which adversely affected their operations."

"The first blacksmith shop thrived intially. Its owner became rich and had a lot of money. Later, he invested it in a big restaurant in the heart of the town. At first, many people came to it and the place was very crowded."

"The owner, who was only a swordsmith, did not know how to serve his clients properly. So, a lot of clients began to get fed up as the place was too busy and crowded, and the unskilled and inactive waiters contributed to its sluggish service. Finally, the number of clients gradually decreased." Otutu explained.

"The business of the restaurant worsened day by day. The owner had to take profits from the sword manufacturing business to continually subsidize the restaurant's operation. Business at the restaurant grew worse and there was no doubt that it also adversely affected the blacksmith's shop, because the owner did not have enough time to take care of its management."

"The quality of the swords was noticeably inferior and he was remonstrated by the palace authorities."

"Many of the orders were canceled. While the restaurant business was precarious, it also caused a negative impact on the progress of the swordsmith's shop."

"The business got worse on both sides, much like a chain reaction," said Otutu and paused to take a sip of water.

"Did you talk or give advice to the first owner?" asked Magga.

"Yes, I did, because we used to be business partners. We consulted with each other many times when we had a problem." Otutu said.

"In the end, the first owner decided to opt for an improvement of the restaurant and expanded it by opening a hotel. Now, the hotel's customers could order food from his restaurant. He told me that this had been his dream since he was young. When he was a boy, he was poor and barely had anything to eat. His food was leftovers from big restaurants. That was why he aspired to own a restaurant so that he would have good food to eat all the time."

"Finally, the owner of the restaurant needed a large sum of money to renovate it as, in reality, he was not good at running it at all. So, he sold me his blacksmith shop in exchange for a great amount of money with the hope that he would be successful again in the restaurant business."

"Is that how your blacksmith shop became the largest one in the town?" Magga was intrigued now.

"Not yet. When I merged the first blacksmith with mine, it was just as big as the other blacksmith. The other one was still large with around 100 workers. Let's go inside and continue our talk after lunch."

In Ancient Egypt, various letters known as Hieroglyphics were created. The above letter corresponds to E in the English alphabet.

In the English alphabet,

the letter E,

as on this coin, means

EXPENSE.

Otutu walked into the sword manufacturing shop, where the laborers were energetically hammering, forging swords, as well as producing spears, short knives, armor plates, metal helmets, chains and shackles.

The crackling of fire in hot furnaces could be heard together with the echoes of hammering in the background.

Otutu then took Magga to the adjacent workshop, where inspection was carried out to ensure the swords' quality before they were packed and delivered to the palace. Many laborers greeted Otutu on the way.

"Young lad, please take a look at the man seated in the corner of the room. He is in charge of packing all the swords before they are delivered to the palace." Otutu said.

"Is he that elegant young man? He looks highly educated," Magga replied.

"Correct. I will tell you his story later this afternoon," said Otutu.

"Take a seat at the reception. Someone will bring us lunch. There I have to finish some work. I'll be back to eat lunch with you."

"Don't worry, sir. Please take all the time you need, I will wait."

When Otutu left, the young man took out a piece of papyrus paper to record the lesson about the first sword maker he had learned from Otutu in the morning:

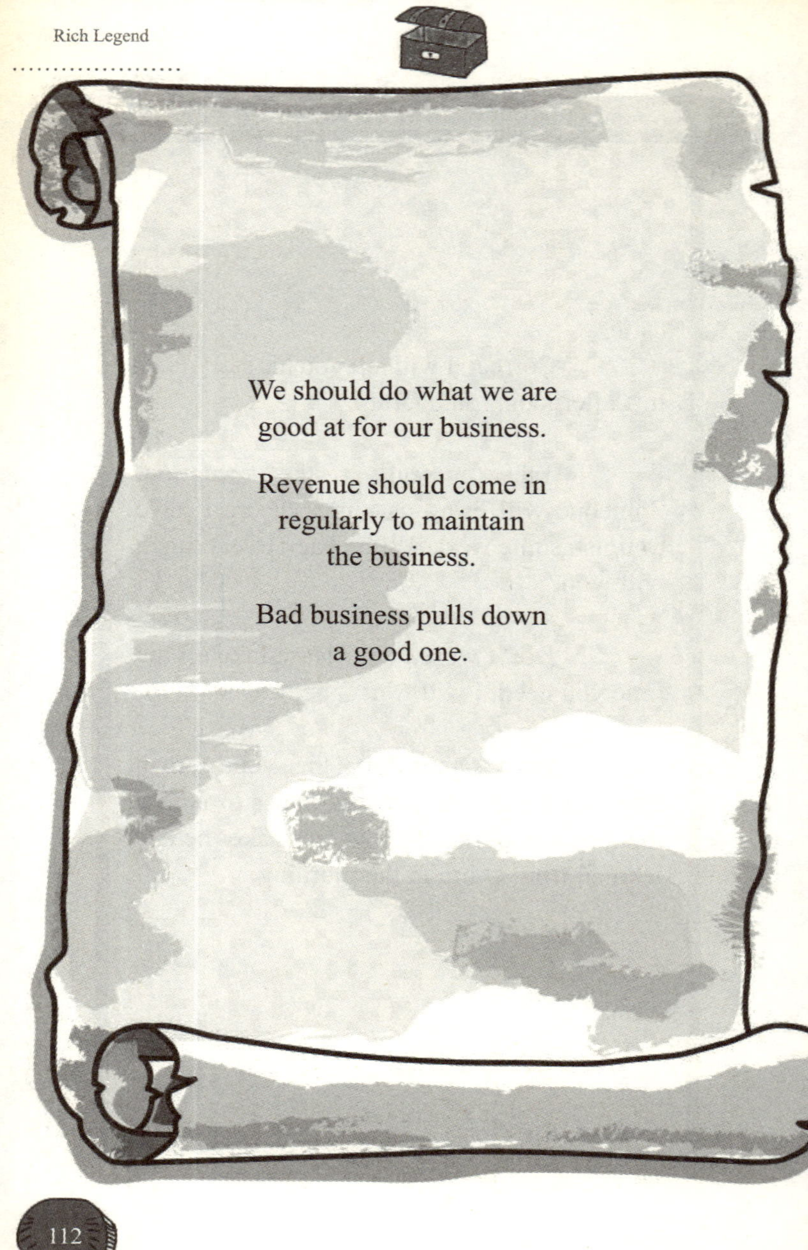

We should do what we are good at for our business.

Revenue should come in regularly to maintain the business.

Bad business pulls down a good one.

Expenses from a bad business,
which cannot subsidize itself,
will doubly affect a good one.

Expenses that exceed revenue
will ultimately cause a business
to collapse.

Suddenly, the door opened and a lot of servants entered with many dishes. Later, Otutu returned.

"I have done what I needed to. Let's have lunch," Otutu offered.

Magga saw that the food millionaires ate was superb. The young man as well as the many servants nearby thought that this was a really delicious and satisfying meal.

After lunch, they headed straight to the reception room where they could observe the laborers from a distance. The sounds of hammering could still be heard such a long way away.

A servant arrived and brought a glass of warm goat milk for Otutu.

"Shall we continue our conversation, young lad?" Otutu asked Magga, who replied.

"Yes, sir"

Otutu said, "We are at the second most successful sword shop. My competitor's shop is twice as wealthy as mine and the first one combined. There are around 100 swordsmiths there. The owner of the second shop is versatile, ingenious and charming to the opposite sex, space."

"Many pretty women want to marry him. Anyway, he has many beautiful wives who he has already married each year. He now has a total of eight women."

"Oh! Eight ladies!" Magga exclaimed.

"He is a millionaire and many men in this town envy that, me included," chuckled Otutu at his joke.

"The second owner of the sword shop is generous, jovial, attractive, good looking, and has a good personality but he also likes to risk a fortune." Otutu explained.

"Does he like gambling, sir?" Magga wondered.

"That's right. Besides his convivial nature and many wives, he also likes drinking and watching camel races," Otutu said.

"He gambles at every kind of game in town. At first, he was fortunate. He won every time. A rumor spread in the village that he has a deity of good luck beside him all the time."

"His business flourished. He married many times as well. His daily life was full of happiness. Until one day when he received an unusually less number of orders because the soldiers of King Pharaoh were mobilized to build the Pyramids and a new palace. The orders for weapons decreased and that adversely affected the revenues of the sword shop. If that was the only reason, the business of the second swordsmith would not be too badly affected. But in reality, the second owner of sword shop had incurred too many expenses, including his eight wives who demanded to be dressed elegantly every day."

"They were none the wiser about the fact that their husband was steadily losing income and had to shoulder the burden of the enormous enterprise, where a 100 swordsmiths worked. In addition, he had to pay a lot of servants."

"Finally, the business started to become critical as the expenses began to exceed the revenues."

"Every wife spent a lot of money on ornaments every day and ate expensive food. Apart from this, each wife had at least four private servants. Besides, there were scores of people the second owner of the sword shop was responsible for. Anyhow, he wanted his wives to be happy and did not want to tell them about the decline in revenues."

"His riches and gold coins reduced considerably. The second shop's owner got drunk every day. Happiness faded. He did not have enough time to oversee his enterprise and the quality of products gradually deteriorated. The swordsmiths had no work to do and got no money. Eventually, they all resigned."

"Thing got worse by the day. It became harder for the wives to get the money they always got so easily. They finally realized the loss of revenues at the business and some of them began to distance themselves from their husband. Some even disappeared without a trace. Slowly, one by one, with him they all left until only the first one remained. She had been with her man the longest. Unlike the other wives, she felt sympathetic for what had happened to her husband."

"After the business deteriorated and the wives left him, he kept on drinking heavily every day and finally, ended up a drunk."

"Worse than that, he was addicted to gambling. While he engaged in betting, he was distracted and momentarily forgot his distress. But unfortunately, he lost the luck he once had."

"Every time he gambled, he lost a great deal of gold coins. He began to borrow gold coins from the owners of the gambling houses and eventually, he was in severe debt."

"The life of the second owner fell to nadir. He needed to repay the debts so he then came to me and asked me to buy his enterprise. After he had paid off all his debts, he began a small business with the money that was left. He continued to live with his first wife, who then gave birth to a son. When their son grew up, the second owner brought his son to work with me."

Otutu paused to drink his glass of warm goat milk. He then said, "Young lad, do you recall the young man you saw at the warehouse inspecting the goods?"

"I remember him. He looked like a well-educated person who came from a noble family," Magga replied.

"That's correct. He is the only son of the blacksmith's first wife. All the man's other children were taken away by their mothers and he was left with no child, except this one," Otutu concluded his story.

"Is that how the first and second sword shops came to belong to you, Otutu?" Magga asked.

"Yes, that is how I've got the largest swordsmith shop in this town," the old man said.

"Were you the sole supplier when the orders for weapons from the palace came?" Magga then asked.

"Sure. My business started with an attempt to survive, then I eventually became secure and wealthy in the end. But some examples of failure could be seen. They always remind me that when a business flourishes, try your best to hold back any excess expenses. If you face a critical situation like less revenue, it will result in a loss due to the expenses exceeding revenue," Otutu continued.

"With regard to personal possessions, gold should be set aside from the business and family affairs. It's just like keeping bags of gold, one on your left and another on your right. Money and gold cannot be mixed together. Money for the family should be used only for the family's needs."

"We should not take money from the enterprise for the family's expense because money in the business must keep flowing all the time, ready to be used to pay for raw materials, minerals, wages of swordsmiths and servants and also general expenses for equipment."

"The owner of an enterprise has to set his own income. He can take what he wants from the business but he needs to fix an amount for his salary. It is not right for him to take money for his own spending whenever he wants by thinking that both bags in his hands are his to spend. People tend to think like this, but it is wrong."

"Young lad, you should remember this story. If you do, the expenses in your business will not create any problems for you in the future," the wise old man added.

"While you have worked, have you always kept your personal expenses and the ones for the enterprise separate?" Magga enquired.

"Yes. I've believed in this principle since the beginning. I always try not to mix the gold coins in my possession. The gold coins of the enterprise will have to be spent on many things. There are a lot of people involved, who need to be paid, such as including buyers, sellers, blacksmiths, shield smiths, metal helmet makers, servants and boys who raise camels, plus plenty of food for all these people."

Money
for the family.

Money for
the enterprise.

A smart entrepreneur must keep his money separate.

Some should be kept as personal pocket money, while the balance should be invested in the organization.

If an entrepreneur cannot keep his money separate, he will soon face financial problems.

"I have a salary and fixed income and spend only what I have. But mostly, I always have some gold coins left in reserve. Every time I get my fixed income, I set aside one gold coin from every ten coins. I do not spend these until I need to."

"Does that mean if you have an income of ten gold coins, you will always save one?" Magga asked inquisitively.

"That's right. If I have an income of 20 gold coins, I will always keep two coins in reserve." Otutu replied.

"Why is that, sir?"

"Everyone tends to have a reason to spend all the gold. Everything seems to be necessary and important," Otutu explained.

"If you are a swordsmith, you will have gold to use until it runs out one day. And you will not have any more left for the future. Even though you might be promoted to a higher position, like a chief swordsmith or even the head of a warehouse, your reasons for spending gold will seem endless."

"You will have more burdens as your career grows. You will have a family, a wife and kids and increased expenses. Besides, you will have to have a house, a majestic camel and servants that attend to you to make your life more comfortable."

"You will eat good food. Your house will become bigger. The number of kids may increase. And when they grow up, they will need to have good education that will make them smarter so that later on, they can successfully serve King Pharaoh."

"It seems that a good career will also increase expenses. So, we need to set aside more gold," Magga added ingeniously.

"Of course. Almost anyone who has an increasing income will also have increasing expenses. Thus, I would like to advise you to set aside one golden coin from the ten. Before spending gold coins you earn, you have to collect one."

"Can I set aside one after I use nine coins?" asked Magga.

"Most people do that but the trap of expenses grows deeper and deeper. Once we plunge into debt, there are no coins left in reserve. Sometimes, it can be worse because you could always incur some unexpected debts," the old man pointed out.

"I will remember your lesson without a doubt. I will set aside one coin from ten that I earn before using them. By doing this will I have plenty of gold coins?" Magga asked.

"Sure, this lesson is just the start of other achievements. If you know how to save your gold coins, you will be one of the top five winners from 100 people." Otutu explained.

When we have ten gold coins,
One must be kept in reserve for emergency use.
One coin.

"After learning about this method of saving gold, I belong to the top five winning groups of 100 people? Ninety five people fall into the trap of expenses, which means people cannot control their expenses because they always find something to spend on, don't they?" Magga asked.

"Mostly, I found only one or two people. I said five at the maximum," the old man replied.

"What should I do with the money I save, sir?" Magga asked.

"The lessons that I have taught you are about expenses and the money saved from the expenses. Regarding saving money tomorrow, Profito will explain to you how to make your savings increase until your gold becomes endless."

"Wow, with your lesson today, I have started to see the path of success so clearly. I cannot wait to see Profito. I better sleep well tonight," Magga said excitedly.

"You certainly are right. My lessons are just the first step to a good start. There are still some more lessons that will play a vital role in the success of your business," Otutu informed Magga.

"Will ask my servant to take you to your lodge. Tomorrow someone will come to take you to see Profito."

"Will I have a chance to see you all again?" Magga asked.

"Certainly, you will see us all on your last day. We will sit together in the same place where you came to see us on your first day." Otutu said.

"I am so grateful for your kindness and I will not forget the lessons you taught me today." Magga said gratefully.

When he arrived at his quarters, the young man felt elated with all the knowledge he had learned and fully realized that sales was not the only think to bring a business prosperity.

Controlling my expenses is another key to help my business become successful. And so is saving one gold coin from ten. I will remember this lesson all my life, because I know it is a good start toward all future successes.

Magga took a bath and came out of his bedroom. It was cold outside. The sky was pitch black, only the shining moon and a 1000 stars could be seen. He was thinking of his home, his elder sister, Moomild, who had been waiting for his return and his younger sister, Minna, who was awaiting his warm hug. Wherever you are in the world, the night sky looks the same everywhere.

The young man fully hoped that his journey to pursue knowledge would help bring more comfort to his life and that of his two sisters.

When we have gold coins, life becomes more comfortable. Our family will have better lives, too.

He then ventured on this long journey to earn gold coins all the time. That was also the question he once asked the millionaire, Ka-Lae.

The right question had allowed Magga to receive the five magical coins that contained a lot of teachings together with a map that led him to meet the three old men.

What he had now acquired from the first two old men was very valuable to his life. Sa-Les had taught him about sales.

The easiest way to earn gold coins is to know your customers and categorize them. We have to know who our customers are, where they are, what they do and how they come to see us. All of these points ignite ways to obtain more income.

Otutu had taught him to oversee the expenses of a business. A real business that gains a large income is necessary to properly control expenses.

The owner of an enterprise should expand his business only if he is good at it. That is another way to keep our gold coins with us for longer. He must know how to efficiently separate his personal bag of gold from the bag of gold for the enterprise.

We should try not to mix them up and we must keep one gold coin from every ten. This is how various expenses will always be proportionally larger in line with the income. Once a business grows and income increases, expenses will increase as well.

The young man made notes of the new knowledge he had acquired from Otutu.

He wrote as he wondered what he would learn the next morning. Everything was so intriguing. He then recorded the following.

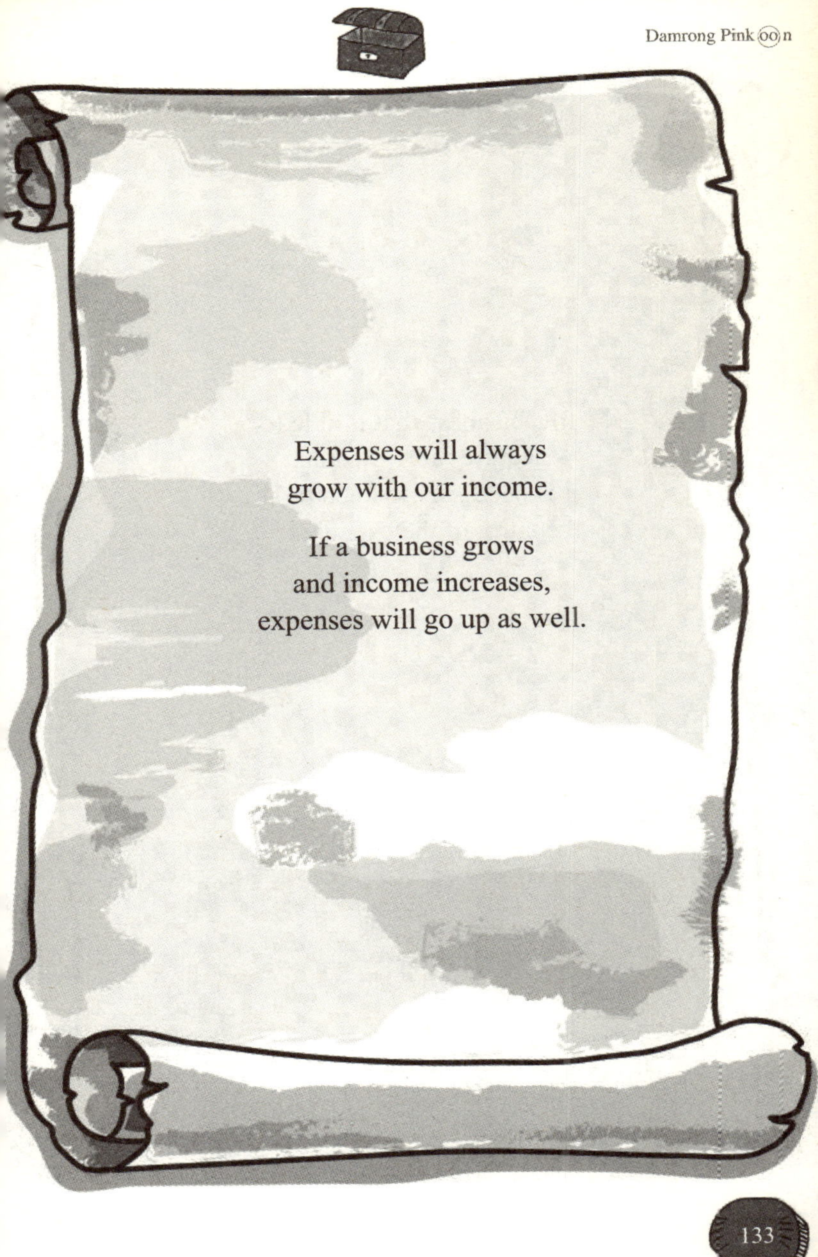

Expenses will always
grow with our income.

If a business grows
and income increases,
expenses will go up as well.

In a business that is able to
acquire more income,
it is necessary to keep tight
control of the expenses.

The owner of the enterprise
should expand his business
only in the field
he is good at
because that means he can keep
gold with him for longer.

Life will be much easier, when we have more gold.

If our wealth increases, our family will also have better lives.

The owner of an enterprise must be able to separate gold into bags. This then has to be used for personal as well as for the enterprise.

Both types of gold have hidden necessary expenses, so they should not be mixed.

We should save one part of gold from ten parts so that we can use it on a rainy day.

In Ancient Egypt, various letters known as

Hieroglyphics were created.

The above letter corresponds

M in the English alphabet.

In the English alphabet,

the letter M,

as on this coin, means

MARKETING.

RICH LEGEND

6

The Third Lesson

is

PROFIT.

The next morning, Magga could not wait to get out of bed, take a bath and get ready for his last appointment. Once he was ready, he went to the balcony and waited for the person assigned by the wise old men to pick him up.

"Are you Magga?" shouted a boy who was leading a camel on a rope.

"Yes, I am," Magga replied excitedly.

"Profito asked me to pick you up from here, sir," the boy explained.

"Thank you very much. I have been waiting for you," Magga said.

They both left the lodge and Magga rode the camel while the boy walked alongside, leading the way.

"Where are we heading?" Magga asked the boy. He did not like it when he did not know where he was going.

"We are going into the town," the boy replied.

"Are we going to Profito's shop?" Magga was curious.

"I do not know how much you know about Profito, but I would like to tell you that in my knowledge, he has never owned a single shop," the boy seems perplaxed.

"So, where are we going now?" Magga still wanted to know.

"We are going to the Profito's house, sir," the boy finally said.

Magga began to feel skeptical about what Otutu had told him. He was sure of the invaluable knowledge he could earn from Profito to make his savings thrive. He didn't he own an enterprise.

"Here we are. This is Profito's house," the boy said.

"This way please," a servant said, who had been expecting the guest in front of the house.

Another person came to welcome him and escort him to the reception room inside the house.

Are we going to Profito's shop?

Profito has never owned any shop.

"Can I ask you something? Were you stationed at the door only to received me?" Magga asked the servant.

"My duty is to welcome every guest of Profito all day long, sir," replied the servant.

"Does that mean people come to see Profito here every day?" Magga asked futher.

"Yes, sir. There are plenty of people who come to see Profito every day. Some arrive with miserable faces but most of them leave smiling and happy. However, some still leave with miserable faces. Apart from these people, there are also many merchants and millionaires in town who also come to see him. They all leave with a smile on their faces and happiness."

"What do they talk about?" Magga wondered aloud.

"I don't know, sir. But Profito will be with you in a few minutes. Now, I have got to leave," the servant said goodbye and left.

"Magga thanked him and continued to wait for Profito."

He was seated in a big hall that was decorated with many ornaments and valuable items, such as golden artifacts, jewelry, engraved gold pieces, sculptures and kitchenware made from real gold. The young man wondered what business Profito was into, because he was clearly so wealthy. He was so deep in his thoughts that he did not realize someone was standing next to him.

"Good morning, young man," Profito greeted Magga.

"Good morning, Profito. I was thinking about something that distracted me so much that I did not see you. Please excuse me," Magga seemed embarrassed to not have noticed the old man arrive.

"It doesn't matter. What do you wish to learn from me? And what did the two old men, Sa-Les and Otutu, tell you?" Profito asked Magga.

"They taught me a lot about sales and how to control expenses and how to save money. Otutu told me that you have a method to make your gold coins thrive for a lifetime. That was why I journeyed to you to understand how you do that, sir."

"A good question deserves a good answer. Well done for a keen ambition to learn things and for coming to find us here." Profito said.

"We are willing to teach those who are interested in tactics to achieve success in business. As for your question, I've rarely heard people ask this question my whole life. But I have given an answer to some people who eventually became millionaires."

"Does it mean that I am not the first one to ask this question, sir?" Magga asked.

"Yes, you are not. Sa-Les and Otutu, as well as the millionaire Ka-Lae from your village, the man who gave you five gold coins and a map, all asked this question to me. And my advice made them very rich."

"You're making me curious, Profito. What do you do that allows you to unravel the puzzles of anyone's business so that they can achieve success?" You've made them all millionaires with countless gold coins," Magga exclaimed.

Magga blurted out what he'd been thinking since the previous night. These included some doubtful thoughts he had heard from both the boy who led his camel and the servant who escorted him into the house. He was also at a loss to understand how the wise old man could unravel the puzzles for so many millionaires. Finally, he could not bear keeping silent and asked all his questions impulsively and in quick succession.

"Slow down, young man. I have more than enough time for you. You will know everything I told the successful millionaires," he said, keen to reassure Magga and calm him down.

"A long time ago, when I was a orphan young boy, I lived under a tree, which served as my refuge. One morning, I woke up and went to work. I earned my living milking goats like every child in the village. I did everything the other children did, such as looking after a herd of cows, buffaloes or cattle. I was also hired to clean the camels of merchants and passers-by."

"I've had the chance to earn my living since I was very young. I also knew how to spend my money. Every time I earned money, I would buy some food to eat and spent the rest on gambling together with my friends. This would not worry me because the next day I could get another job and earn more tiny pieces of gold to buy food again." Profito explained.

"That is what the kids do in my town too. Children hire themselves out for every kind of job. But I do not see any difference between you and the others," Magga said.

Profito smiled and continued, “Then came the day that changed my life. One morning, when I woke up. I felt ill. I could not move my body. All I could do was lay in one place, very still, for many hours.”

“Fortunately, I laid down under a big tree whose branches shaded me from the burning sun. I was thirsty and hungry. I lost consciousness several times and awoke again but still could not move my body,” the wise old man explained.

“Didn’t anybody look after you, sir?” Magga asked.

“No, I was an orphan. My friends took my jobs and did the work I would have done. When I was not present, it meant that they had one competitor less, it was good for them.”

"I finally woke up because I was hungry and thirsty. When the sun went down, I began to feel better. I felt as if I was dreaming and I had floated up into the air. My body felt light and comfortable, as it was floating in the sky. All of a sudden, golden beams of light came out the moon and all the stars in the sky."

"Then a voice came from the golden beams of light that I remember very well. I won't forget it for as long as I live. The voice said to me:"

"Kid, you must learn to save some gold and make it grow."

"You must collect gold and make it increase every day."

"Become smart and use the gold you earn to make an interest return out of it."

"Gold will always be true to you if you know how to keep it."

"Kid, you must learn to save some gold and make it grow."

"That was the last voice I heard before I regained consciousness the next morning." Profito went on.

"The following morning, I was conscious again and felt no pain. I had come back to life again. Then, I went to ask for water and food from the person who hired me to look after the cattle on his farm. Before I started to work again to pay back that meal, I remembered my dream."

"Since I never had gold and was still a little boy, it did not concern me. However, afterwards, I made my first attempt to save money in exchange for gold and I was willing to proceed as advised."

"One day, I noticed I had collected enough money to exchange it for gold. I had planned to visit Aunty Antus that day. I went to her food shop and handed over a bag of gold to her. I had saved it from months and I now knew that she was in trouble."

Little Profito had said to Aunty Antus, "I have five gold coins. I don't know how many you need. This is all I have saved. I would like to give it to you as a token of your kindness for giving me food over the years."

Little Profito had the naivety of a child and lacked any experience in trading.

Aunty Antus had said, "Little Profito, I am thankful to you. I can't take all your gold as it is worth more than all the food I have ever given to you. So, let's do like this. I will borrow two of your gold coins and I will return them to you when I can. But if I can't return, I will pay you an interest fee every ten days. I will give you one-tenth of these two gold coins."

"So, I gave her two gold coins and kept the other three with me." Profito said.

*Please come to take
an interest fee of one-tenth
from the total owed
every ten days.*

"In fact, I had no idea and could not figure out what an interest fee meant. I just wanted to help the one person who helped me to survive when I was starving. Besides, she took good care of me as if I was one of her kids. I too needed love and warmth."

Before I left, Aunty Antus said to me, "I never imagined that a little boy like you would be able to amass such a lot of gold. I think you must have put all your efforts in to doing this, I am proud of you. I appreciate the goodwill you have shown to me and my family. I promise to return your two gold coins as soon as I can. Please come to visit me every ten days so that you can get an interest fee of one-tenth of the total value," Aunty Antus had felt grateful and promised to return the money plus interest of one-tenth from the total two gold coins.

Profito then said, "Ten days later, I went to see Aunty Antus received the interest as she promised. That was when I realized what it meant. After that, I went to see Aunty Antus every ten days and received an interest payment from her.

That is when I knew instantly that gold could bear offsprings.

I kept on working and I amassed gold without any precise aim. One year passed, and I continued to receive interest from Aunty Antus. After all that time, she then finally returned the two gold coins to me. Then I counted all the coins in my possession to be 12 in number.

Aunty Antus was grateful to me for helping her enterprise survive critical financial difficulties. She told her neighbors in the village about my virtues and many appreciated it. Some merchants wished to borrow gold to extend their funds.

Some asked me for five or ten coins at a time, and some even asked for 50, but I told them that I only had 12. The big merchants left and I could give two coins each at the most. After everyone had left, I worked out that I had lent coins to five people and kept two for myself. Still some merchants came and asked for my 2 coins, but I declined. I would surely have had nothing left if my bag of gold was empty.

Those five merchants gave me the same promise as Aunty Antus. They would give me interest of one-tenth from the two coins every ten days."

"I was very lucky because everyone kept their promise. In only ten days, the gold I had lent to the five merchants, two coins each, bore offsprings of one coin!"

"In one year, 12 golden coins that I loaned turned into 50 gold coins."

"People constantly came to ask me for a loan and I grew up to be the youngest and wealthiest man in the village. Big and small merchants kept coming to borrow my money and they also paid me interest every ten days. My gold continued to bear me offsprings." Profito explained his trick.

"Has anyone ever failed to return or repay the gold or interest to you in all these years?" Magga interrupted.

"Of course. Some merchants were not good at business. Some of them were good at hunting but embarked on selling clothes, food or goat milk and in the end they failed. So my gold was wasted in their unsuccessful ventures." Profito explained.

I want to borrow two coins but you cannot give them to me. Why are you so unsympathetic?

I am sorry. I really cannot lend them to you. I have only two coins left with me now.

"Weren't you sorry, sir, Magga asked."

Profito quickly said, "I had my criteria on how I distributed the volume of golden coins and how many could be lent. I also took into account the requirement of each type of business, including the character of the merchant in question. Not all of them could keep their words despite being good people."

"Those who did not repay me could neither find enough gold to return nor pay the interest. I didn't know what to do. Some said that they had only their life left; no business and no gold. I had no way but to write off the debts."

"Anyway, I soon realized that it was me who needed to analyze my business instead of them. I then started to study and dig deep into their businesses. I noticed that some enterprises looked prosperous and promising but they lacked sufficient funds. Some businesses looked unlikely to survive a financial crisis in a short period of time, thus I could not take a risk to grant them a huge loan of gold."

"Well, Magga, do you recall the business of Otutu? He took over the enterprise of the first swordsmith and not long afterwards the second swordsmith also sold his enterprise to him." Profito asked.

"I remember, sir. Otutu told me this story only yesterday." Magga explained.

"Otutu came to ask me for a loan of gold to buy the second swordsmith's shop. He needed a whole lot of gold this time."

"You lent him the gold, right?" asked Magga.

"I did more than that. Instead of lending him the gold, I decided to invest in Otutu's venture. I'd already analyzed that the majority of his income was derived from the palace which paid on time and gave precise orders without breaking its promises. If I invested with Otutu, I would have far more income than the interest I received. I did not hesitate to bring my big gold bullion to invest with him in view of his respectable behavior and character. He knows how to control expenses and to make profits soar in a business enterprise. So I entrusted my gold with him." Profito gave the story.

"And did you get gold worthier than one-tenth of interest, sir?" Magga was curious to know.

"It was many times more than that. Otutu is an honest, frugal and punctual man. Every year, I receive a handsome return of gold from this joint investment with him."

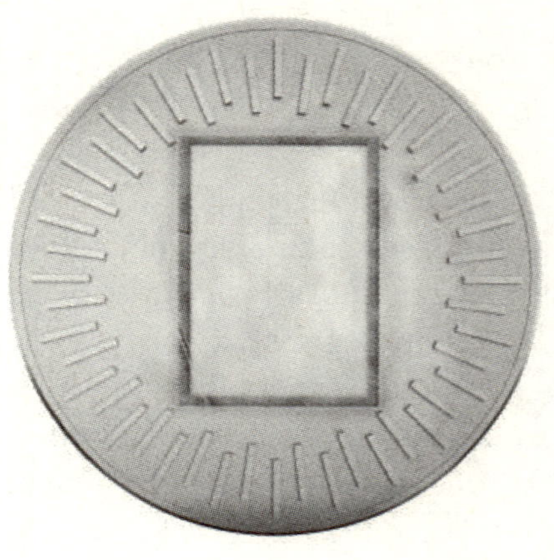

In Ancient Egypt, various letters known as

Hieroglyphics were created.

The letter above corresponds

P in the English alphabet.

In the English alphabet,

the letter P as

on this coin means,

PROFIT.

"I invested my gold in many enterprises both in my town and in the neighboring ones. You have to learn the character of each entrepreneur you invest in. If not, everything you loan will be gone and you'll never get it back whether their enterprises are good or bad."

Magga was well aware of the ingenuity of Profito and acknowledged his success. In addition, he appreciated Profito's time in teaching him.

"Nowadays, there are many wealthy merchants and some of them want their money to grow. So, they deposit their gold with me and I look for those who want to borrow it. Then, I hand over the interest back to the merchants. They also give me a handsome return, which is beneficial to both of us." Profito said.

Magga had truly learned a lot. He said gratefully, "I came to meet the right person, sir. You have helped me tremendously. I can now solve the puzzles of how to run a successful business. I will remember what you have taught me all my life."

"And will you go back home now?" the old man asked.

"Soon, sir. But first I will make a record of today's lessons before I forget them."

"Good. Could you please give the millionaire Ka-Lae a souvenir from me?" Profito asked.

"Yes, sir, with pleasure," Magga was more than happy to help.

Profito is an enterprising merchant who knows how to invest his profits so that he can continually earn gold. He had successfully turned a small amount of money into many bullions of gold. He is such an ingenious millionaire that he successfully made money bear offsprings without owning any enterprise. He knows an efficient way to invest his money by analyzing other enterprises that yield good returns and then he invests his money in them. At the same time, he also lends gold to other enterprises from which he expects to receive a high interest.

Profito handed Magga something and said, "These are five coins that bear the new symbols that I wish to give Ka-Lae and also to you. You will soon become a millionaire in your town."

"How do you know I will become successful?" Magga seemed surprised.

"I can see curiosity in your eyes to run a successful business. You have the determination to be wealthy and you possess the aspiration to succeed. I have also noticed your glowing resolution; it is the same as I saw in Sa-Les, Otutu and the millionaire Ka-lae. They all have the same firm determination. I hope that you make it in your own business."

"Thank you very much, Profito. I will come back to see you again when I am successful in my business," Magga said with delight

The young man returned to the guesthouse just before sunset. He took out a piece of papyrus paper to record the eventful day; he wrote:

Use your gold savings
and make them multiply.

Invest your gold in a lucrative business that will yield steady revenues and controllable expenses.

Don't invest your gold till
all of it gets over.

Don't let a single person monopolize your money.

Spread the risk of losing your gold by putting it in as many places as possible.

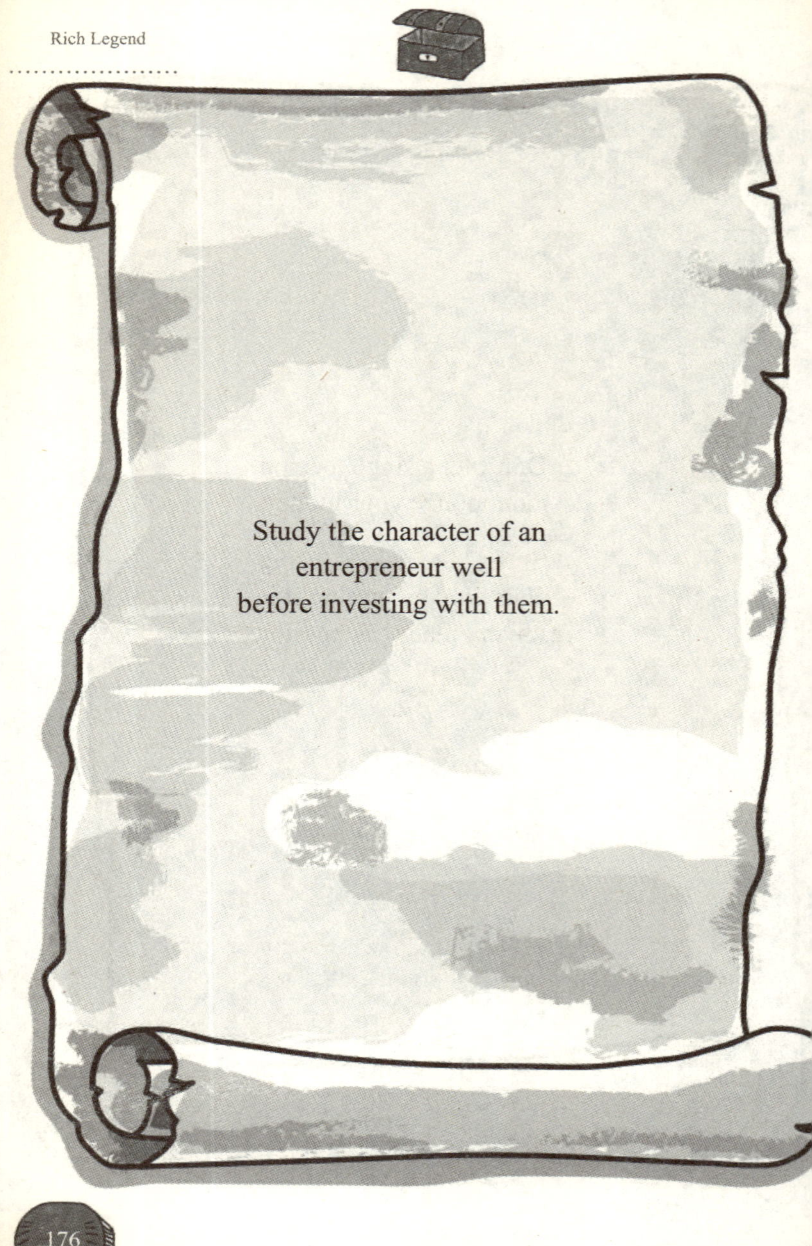
Study the character of an
entrepreneur well
before investing with them.

Smart investors always analyze each enterprise themselves.

Don't believe in anyone who is not good at analyzing their business.

RICH LEGEND

7

The Last Lesson

from

the Three Old Men.

Magga awoke the next morning and felt refreshed. He was ready to go to see the three old men. He would go to the same place as the first time when he had arrived.

“Good morning, Magga. Did you sleep well last night?” enquired Sa-Les on seeing him.

“Yes, I did. You must have all woken up very early, sir,” Magga asked him.

“We are old. We go to bed early so we wake up early too,” responded the old man Sa-Les with a smile. “We would now like to see you off.”

“I actually do not want to go home, Magga said, I still want to know a lot of things and I have so many questions to ask each of you.”

“We have already advised you on everything you need to know. You gathered all the knowledge that has been derived from our lifetime experiences. Your questions or queries are all real-life cases that you will have to deal with. You can apply the knowledge you’ve gathered from us as guidelines in operating your business.”

"You should always remember the principles you have learned and closely follow them. That's all we can offer. Anyway, regarding the other questions, it is necessary to leave the decision-making to talented entrepreneurs who can tackle these problems."

"Believe me, Magga, you are a good person with firm conviction, your wise decisions will help you survive any future crisis."

"Lastly, we all wish you good luck, success in your business and a happy family life. Please come back someday to visit us when you become a millionaire." Sa-Les finally said.

"When will I become a millionaire, sir?" Magga asked one more question. Sorry, I mean, how much gold should I have?"

"Just know the word enough in your life and then you will become a millionaire immediately," the wise Profito answered.

"Yes, that's right, whenever you are satisfied with what you have, you will become physically and mentally happy. Everyone can do that but few people really understand the point. One day, you will fully understand the meaning of the word enough.

"Can I ask you another question, please?"

"Sure," one of the old men said.

"Why did it take the millionaire Ka-Lae about seven or eight years to meet you and learn your knowledge before he returned to our town, whereas I have only spent half a year on my jouney and learned all this in a few days?"

"It was kind of Ka-Lae to give you the map that made it easy for you to reach this destination and meet us."

This situation is similar to running a business. You must know your destination before you start. By doing this, you will not waste your time and energy. You will reach your destination faster without getting lost.

*Only when you know the meaning of the word **enough**,*

you will become a millionaire immediately.

"The millionaire, Ka-Lae traveled to many cities. He had crossed mountains, streams and met many thinkers, calculators and theorists but he did not get the answer he wanted. Finally, he came to us with firm determination and enthusiasm like you. We spent the same amount of time with him as we have with you; just a few days." Sa-Les explained.

"I feel fortunate to have met you all and to have had the opportunity to learn so much," added the young man.

"Few people will have the opportunity to learn from three masters like you did. You are magicians for the millionaire Ka-Lae and me." Magga said, overwhelmed with bliss at the rare chance to learn important lessons from the three veteran men.

Only a few people are lucky to learn these secret business methods and Magga was impressed by the personalities of the three old men. He wanted to say thank you a 1000 times to them because these lessons were invaluable. The knowledge that he acquired in a few days could now be applied to all his businesses throughout his life.

"About these five coins with the new symbols, please keep them safe. If destiny wishes, we will surely meet again," Otutu said as he bade farewell to Magga and gave him the five coins with the brand new styles.

"I sincerely bid you farewell. I would like to express my heartfelt gratitude to the three of you and I will come back to visit you again." Magga said.

"Goodbye, young man," said the three wise men.

The young man mounted his camel and left the Pund region. He headed back towards his village where his sisters were waiting for him.

After he returned home, he did business according to the methods and principles he had learned from the three wise man.

Finally, he was doing business with an understanding of its essence.

He did business as if

he had been doing it for years.

It was now a part of him.

RICH LEGEND

8

Five Coins.

Then,

10

years

later,

There were three knocks on the door and two calls of millionaire Magga's name.

"May I know what is your business with the millionaire?" asked a servant.

"My name is Glosstie, I would like to consult the millionaire Magga, sir."

"What has happened, young man?" Magga said as he walked over to greet his visitor.

"I have considerable difficulties with my business. I would like to learn how I can earn gold coins all the time. I've heard a widespread rumor from the villagers that you know how to achieve this," Glosstie quickly asked.

"Wait a minute." Magga walked back to where he had come from and returned with a box. It looked like a small treasure case.

"Follow the map inside and bring back the five symbols from the three magicians you will meet at the end of your journey. Then, you will know the answers to all your questions. Your gold will grow endlessly." Magga said.

"I am grateful to you, sir. I will set out immediately once I bid farewell to my parents and relatives."

"Could you convey a message from me to the three old men? Tell them that I miss them very much. Also, tell them that I have understood what enough means."

"I will follow your instructions, sir." Glosstie finally said.

"I wish you good luck." Magga smiled at him and said.

When we do not know our precise destination, we are likely to get lost and waste precious time on the journey.

To do business,
we must know our
precise destination
before starting our journey.

If you understand the word enough,
you are bound to become a millionaire.

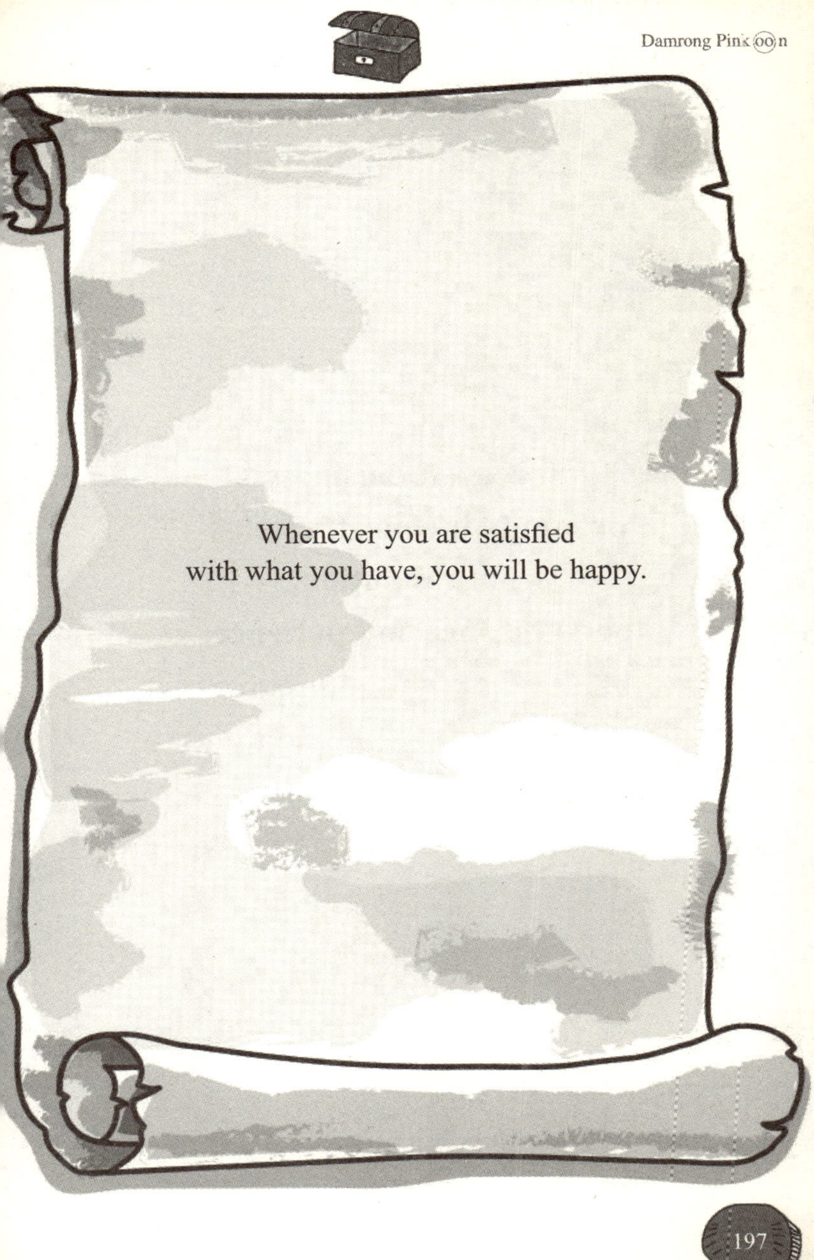
Whenever you are satisfied
with what you have, you will be happy.

Success in business
or family life mostly stems
from resolution,
perseverance and patience.

Fortune is likely to favor
only the ones
who are intent at their work.

DAMRONG PINKOON was born in Bangkok, Thailand, in November1972. He graduated with a Bachelor's Degree in Business Administration and a Marketing Major from The University of Thai Chamber of Commerce, Bangkok, Thailand (UTCC). He also attended the College of Management of Mahidol University (CMMU) from where he graduated with a Master's Degree in Management.

DAMRONG PINKOON started working with Thai Carbon Black Public Company Limited (Birla Group from India) and then moved to Thai Escorp Limited, a Japanese company based in Bangkok, Thailand with its headquarters in Shinsho Corporation in Tokyo, Japan.

DAMRONG PINKOON started his own business in Bangkok in 1999 called "Rester Massage Chair" when he was 26 years old. He was a successful business man and his business became talk of the town within four years and today is one of the most successful businesses in the luxury seating sector.

After tasting success in business, he began writing many pocket books which became bestsellers in his hometown. As a well-known author, he was invited to speak at seminars, advised other corporations and individuals and became an instructor of business strategies.

His philosophy books and how-to novels have been translated into many languages in the past few years and have since gone on to be bestsellers on the international book scene.

Damrong Pinkoon

Special Thanks

Ms. Sirisara Pinkoon	**for all the support**
Ms. Daranee Rattanathum	**forassistingandcorroborating**
Ms. Chompoo Trakullersathien	**for translation**
Mr. Philip Hall	**for editing**
Ms. Uchenee Puttichard	**for assisting**

And thanks again for everything
I've learned from all my professors.
And to the great writers who wrote great books,
thank you for making it all possible for me.

RICH LEGEND

UK 1st Print in June 2014

United Kingdom Distributor
Star Book Sales
www.starbooksales.com

....

India Distributor
Jaico Publishing House
www.jaicopub.com

....

Brazil Distributor
Universo Dos Livros
www.universodoslivros.com.br

....

South Korea Distributor
Amo Agency
www.amoagency.com

....

Czech Distributor
Anahitac
www.anahitacz.cz

....

Kindle Application
Amazon
www.Amazon.com
search : Damrong Pinkoon

....

Nook Application
Barnes & Noble
www.barnesandnoble.com
search : Damrong Pinkoon

....

Damrong Pinkoon Application
iPad + iPhone + Google Play + Android
Search : Damrong Pinkoon

....